SELECTOR®
actualidad editorial

Doctor Erazo 120 Colonia Doctores México 06720, D.F.
Tel. (52 55) 51 34 05 70 Fax. (52 55) 57 61 57 16

TOEFL -EJERCICIOS PRÁCTICOS PARA EL EXAMEN-
Autor: Víctor Hugo Chávez
Colección: Didáctica

Diseño de portada: Carlos Varela

D.R. © Selector, S.A. de C.V., 2007
        Doctor Erazo, 120, Col. Doctores
        C.P. 06720, México, D.F.

ISBN 10: 970-643-907-2
ISBN 13: 978-970-643-907-9

Cuarta reimpresión Abril 2011

	Sistema de clasificación Melvil Dewey
420	
C15	
2007	Chávez, Víctor Hugo.
	TOEFL -Ejercicios prácticos para el examen- /
	Víctor Hugo Chávez.--
	Cd. de México, México: Selector, 2007.
	128 p.
	ISBN 10: 970-643-907-2
	ISBN 13: 978-970-643-907-9
	1. Didáctica. 2. Enseñanza de idioma inglés

Víctor Hugo Chávez

TOEFL

Ejercicios prácticos para el examen

SELECTOR
actualidad editorial

Contenido

Introducción 7

Section A
Exercises 001-240 11

Section B
Exercises 241-400 73

Answer key 117

El examen TOEFL se ha convertido en el estándar que usan las escuelas y las empresas para medir el nivel de dominio del inglés. Los resultados de este examen definen la admisión a las mejores universidades o preparatorias. También suelen determinar qué personas obtendrán los trabajos mejor remunerados. De la misma manera, muchas empresas lo usan para seleccionar los empleados que obtendrán un ascenso, un aumento de sueldo o un bono.

El uso generalizado de este examen crea la necesidad de desarrollar métodos de estudio alternativos y complementarios más flexibles, es decir, que se ajusten a una gama más amplia de requerimientos y presupuestos. Los métodos tradicionales son muy caros e inflexibles, además de que no cuentan con suficientes ejercicios de práctica que se puedan realizar a cualquier hora y en cualquier lugar, sin necesidad de asistir a una costosa clase especializada.

Con el fin de proporcionar más herramientas y opciones de estudio que estén al alcance de todos, hemos desarrollado este libro de ejercicios prácticos. Es el complemento perfecto para cualquier programa de preparación TOEFL. Los 400 ejercicios de opción múltiple le permitirán detectar de manera inmediata las áreas más deficientes en su dominio del inglés. Lo puede llevar a donde quiera y lo puede usar donde quiera (el autobús, la oficina, la casa), en cualquier momento que tenga disponible.

El libro se divide en tres secciones. La primera contiene ejercicios en los que usted deberá escoger la respuesta que debe ir en el espacio en blanco para completar la frase. En la segunda sección deberá elegir la respuesta que tenga el significado más cercano a la frase original. La tercera sección contiene las respuestas. Así de fácil. No necesitará más instrucciones.

Nos es muy grato poder ofrecerle una herramienta de estudio que es capaz de ajustarse a las necesidades de cualquier persona.

Section A

Circle the correct answer (001-240)

001   The police carried out a _____ investigation.
     a)   thorough
     b)   though
     c)   thought
     d)   tough

002   Lisa was fond of John, _____ he often annoyed her.
     a)   thorough
     b)   though
     c)   thought
     d)   tough

003   He had _____ very deeply about the problem.
     a)   thorough
     b)   though
     c)   thought
     d)   tough

004   It can be _____ trying to juggle a career and a family.
   a) thorough
   b) though
   c) thought
   d) tough

005   The matter came _____ at the last meeting.
   a) up
   b) over
   c) in
   d) on

006   Mexico is rich _____ oil.
   a) on
   b) in
   c) with
   d) over

007   Tom ended _____ in jail.
   a) over
   b) away
   c) down
   d) up

008   The handle fell _____.
    a) away
    b) up
    c) off
    d) over

009   John, who should really know better, _____ came
to the meeting unprepared.
    a) appear
    b) apparently
    c) apparent
    d) appearance

010   Mr. Jones is highly _____ for his skill at negotiating
contracts.
    a) suspected
    b) respected
    c) inspected
    d) expected

011   All our bank managers are _____ to approve loans
of up to $20,000.
    a) authority
    b) authoritative
    c) authorize
    d) authorized

012   I was very angry because Mark _____ me when I
       was trying to work.
       a) displayed
       b) discarded
       c) discounted
       d) disturbed

013   It's hot inside. Take _____ your jacket.
       a) out
       b) off
       c) away
       d) on

014   The doctor advised her _____ smoking.
       a) against
       b) about
       c) no
       d) not

015   We were tied _____ in traffic.
       a) off
       b) out
       c) over
       d) up

016   They came back _____ car.
    a) on
    b) in
    c) by
    d) with

017   The lawyer handed _____ the letter to sign just as
    I was leaving.
    a) my
    b) mine
    c) I
    d) me

018   What I want to know is _____ car is blocking mine!
    a) that
    b) why
    c) whose
    d) when

019   I couldn't carry all the bags _____ so I got a porter
    to help me.
    a) myself
    b) mine
    c) my
    d) me

020   If I had been invited to make a speech, I _____ happy to.
a)   am
b)   will be
c)   would've been
d)   would be

021   The bank has agreed to _____ me some money.
a)   borrow
b)   lease
c)   lend
d)   grant

022   We were waiting for him but he didn't show _____.
a)   in
b)   on
c)   up
d)   at

023   I read the article _____ the newspaper.
a)   in
b)   on
c)   over
d)   at

024 To start _____, we don't have enough money.
a) about
b) in
c) on
d) with

025 He is _____ trying to contact his office, but so far he hasn't been successful.
a) almost
b) yet
c) still
d) never

026 Let's _____ a cup of coffee before we get back to work.
a) have
b) to have
c) having
d) taking

027 I would like to join you for dinner, _____, I'm not sure I can.
a) therefore
b) so
c) unless
d) however

028   Joe doesn't have _____ to invest.
    a)   many
    b)   mostly
    c)   much
    d)   very

029   The plane took _____.
    a)   away
    b)   up
    c)   off
    d)   over

030   Have you got it sorted _____ ?
    a)   by
    b)   on
    c)   in
    d)   out

031   Don't ask _____ trouble.
    a)   in
    b)   for
    c)   to
    d)   on

032 They sell the eggs _____ the dozen.
   a) by
   b) in
   c) on
   d) at

033 You have to have your car serviced regularly, _____ ,
   the warranty will become invalid.
   a) still
   b) nevertheless
   c) otherwise
   d) consequently

034 I expect you to visit all the major wholesalers in the area,
   _____ , you should visit several retail outlets.
   a) in accordance
   b) in addition
   c) in brief
   d) in respect to

035 The coach made the students _____ very hard.
   a) to practice
   b) practicing
   c) practiced
   d) practice

036   Even though it was snowing, there was very _____ ice on the road.
a) many
b) less
c) little
d) few

037   The drain is _____ by mud.
a) blocked in
b) filled in
c) blocked up
d) stopped

038   Your name is _____ the top of the list.
a) on
b) in
c) over
d) at

039   She blew _____ the candles.
a) out
b) over
c) off
d) away

040   I was late because my car broke _____.
   a) over
   b) down
   c) out
   d) off

041   He traveled _____ 7:45 train, which arrived at 8:30.
   a) in the
   b) on the
   c) by the
   d) by

042   I saw Peter _____ a concert last Friday.
   a) at
   b) on
   c) in
   d) by

043   Our department is _____ the second floor of the building.
   a) over
   b) at
   c) on
   d) in

044   I'm going away _____ the end of March.
- a) on
- b) in
- c) for
- d) at

045   Two _____ four equals eight.
- a) multiplied
- b) by
- c) times
- d) plus

046   Six _____ four equals ten.
- a) add
- b) plus
- c) more
- d) added

047   Nine _____ two equals seven.
- a) minus
- b) less
- c) minor
- d) lost

048   Six divided _____ two equals three.
a) over
b) in
c) on
d) by

049   The more electricity you use, _____.
a) your bill will be higher
b) will be higher your bill
c) the higher your bill will be
d) higher will be your bill

050   The exam was _____ we expected.
a) more easy that
b) easier than
c) more easy than
d) easier as

051   I haven't got _____ on holiday at the moment.
a) money enough to go
b) enough money to go
c) money enough for going
d) enough money when going

052   Jim _____ to find a job but he had no luck.
   a) tried hard
   b) tried hardly
   c) hardly tried
   d) try hard

053   The company didn't find out he was stealing. He got
   _____ with it.
   a) on
   b) by
   c) away
   d) over

054   He escaped from prison. The police are _____
   him.
   a) after
   b) by
   c) at
   d) in

055   He got _____ the plane.
   a) outside
   b) away
   c) out
   d) off

056   Your car is too old. Get _____ it.
    a)   away from
    b)   out of
    c)   rid of
    d)   another of

057   There's a cherry _____ of the glass.
    a)   at the end
    b)   on the lower part
    c)   at the bottom
    d)   on the end

058   The children are well cared _____.
    a)   about
    b)   of
    c)   in
    d)   for

059   Go ahead, I'll _____.
    a)   catch up you
    b)   catch you up
    c)   catch on you
    d)   catch you in

060   The label came _____.
   a) off
   b) over
   c) away
   d) on

061   Melvyn has been working here _____.
   a) about two years
   b) for two years
   c) since two years
   d) two years ago

062   Where's the book I gave you? What _____ with it?
   a) was done
   b) have you done
   c) have you been done
   d) had been done

063   Patrick has lost his keys again. It's the second time this
       _____ ?
   a) is happening
   b) happen
   c) had happened
   d) has happened

064   Opinion is split on _____ the problem is more than symbolic.
a) whether
b) if
c) when
d) therefore

065   I think taxes are too high. I'm _____ a new tax cut.
a) by
b) on
c) with
d) for

066   Are you for or _____ me?
a) against
b) over
c) with
d) on

067   The teenagers were hanging _____ the mall.
a) over
b) around
c) to
d) inside

068   I don't believe it. I want to see it _____.
   a) on myself
   b) by myself
   c) for myself
   d) with myself

069   If you want a bigger apartment, you _____ to pay
      more.
   a) had
   b) would have
   c) would have had
   d) will have

070   Several passengers were _____ in the train crash.
   a) injured
   b) damaged
   c) destroyed
   d) inflicted

071   I _____ his views on the matter.
   a) agreed to
   b) agreed with
   c) consented to
   d) admitted on

072 _____ of this will stop the flow of migrants.
    a) Nor
    b) None
    c) No
    d) Nothing

073 Nancy wasn't tired, _____ she hadn't slept for a very long time.
    a) nevertheless
    b) despite
    c) however
    d) though

074 _____ his anxiety, Norman was able to concentrate.
    a) Though
    b) However
    c) Despite
    d) Nevertheless

075 _____ a car when they were living in Houston?
    a) Had they
    b) Did they have
    c) Were they having
    d) Do they had

076 The guy sitting next to me on the plane was nervous because he _____ before.
a) hasn't flown
b) didn't fly
c) wasn't flying
d) hadn't flown

077 They ask me to copy the reports, but I told them to do it _____.
a) himself
b) themselves
c) myself
d) yourselves

078 The situation _____ that he resign.
a) commands
b) orders
c) demands
d) wants

079 We don't back _____ from risk, we embrace it.
a) down
b) out
c) up
d) over

080 This motel has many vacant _____.
    a) places
    b) pieces
    c) parts
    d) units

081 Thank you, I'll make it _____ to you.
    a) on
    b) up
    c) in
    d) over

082 What was wrong with you? Why _____ go to the hospital?
    a) had you to
    b) could you
    c) did you have to
    d) must you

083 I've lost my pen. I _____ it somewhere.
    a) must have dropped
    b) must drop
    c) must have been dropping
    d) must be dropping

084   Why did you stay at a hotel when you went to Chicago?
       You _____ with Tom.
       a) may stay
       b) can stay
       c) could stay
       d) could have stayed

085   She wanted to cry but she managed to hold _____
       her tears.
       a) back
       b) inside
       c) on
       d) over

086   What's the Spanish _____ "car" ?
       a) of
       b) in
       c) with
       d) for

087   This house is _____.
       a) on sell
       b) for sale
       c) for sell
       d) in sale

088   They ate all the snacks. There was nothing _____.
a)   over left
b)   to leave
c)   left over
d)   over

089   The bus _____ arrive at noon but it was an hour late.
a)   is supposed to
b)   supposed to
c)   isn't supposed to
d)   was supposed to

090   There's somebody walking behind us. I think _____.
a)   we are following
b)   we are being followed
c)   we are followed
d)   we were being followed

091   Where _____ ?   In Boston.
a)   were you born
b)   are you born
c)   have you been born
d)   did you born

33

092   We _____ by a loud noise last night.
    a) woke up
    b) are woken up
    c) were woken up
    d) were waking up

093   Did you _____ the door?
    a) lock
    b) luck
    c) lack
    d) lick

094   I hope you can _____ us for dinner while you're in town.
    a) join
    b) enjoy
    c) look forward to
    d) intend

095   The chief administrator of the airport announced that there were plans to _____ the main runway.
    a) long
    b) length
    c) lengthen
    d) lengthened

096   As of this morning, the _____ of the burglar who robbed First Interstate Bank's main branch was still unclear.
   a) identify
   b) identity
   c) identification
   d) identifying

097   Teachers must _____ their students on academic matters.
   a) advice
   b) attend
   c) listen
   d) advise

098   Her Halloween _____ was very elaborate.
   a) disguising
   b) custom
   c) disguised
   d) costume

099   I'm sure I locked the door. I clearly remember _____ it.
   a) having lock
   b) locking
   c) to lock
   d) locked

100   I must go now. I promised _____ late.
  a) not being
  b) I shouldn't be
  c) not to be
  d) to not be

101   Her belt was so _____ that it fell off.
  a) loose
  b) loss
  c) lose
  d) lost

102   He is very intelligent and _____ in his field.
  a) knowing
  b) knew
  c) knowledge
  d) knowledgeable

103   Tom Allen _____ in Colorado since he was a child.
  a) will live
  b) lives
  c) is living
  d) has been living

104 May I _____ your dictionary for a moment?
   a) take over
   b) lend
   c) borrow
   d) get

105 That wasn't a _____ thing to do.
   a) wisely
   b) wise
   c) wised
   d) wising

106 Don't worry. I can see just _____, thanks.
   a) well
   b) now
   c) nice
   d) fine

107 I don't want to know. Please _____ it to yourself.
   a) tell
   b) get
   c) take
   d) keep

108   When Lisa came to London, she had to get used
       _____ on the left.
       a)   to driving
       b)   to drive
       c)   driving
       d)   about driving

109   He was warned _____ late again.
       a)   not being
       b)   not to be
       c)   don't be
       d)   not been

110   The manager asked me to _____ our customers to
       see how they liked our products.
       a)   review
       b)   revise
       c)   revisit
       d)   reveal

111   Don't insist. It's _____of the question.
       a)   not
       b)   part
       c)   none
       d)   out

112 Our plans fell _____ when it began to rain.
a) away
b) through
c) over
d) down

113 It took us quite a long time to get here. It was _____ journey.
a) three hour
b) the three-hours
c) a three-hours
d) a three-hour

114 When _____ invented?
a) was telephone
b) were telephones
c) was the telephone
d) were the telephones

115 There are millions of stars in _____.
a) our space
b) space
c) a space
d) the space

116   Sean is not going with us. He changed his _____.
    a) thought
    b) way
    c) mind
    d) opinion

117   You cheated. It's not _____.
    a) fair
    b) fared
    c) fare
    d) faired

118   The president appealed to the general _____ for
support.
    a) people
    b) populated
    c) public
    d) population

119   The Royal Packing Company, _____ is located in
Phoenix, is the second biggest packing company in the
west.
    a) that
    b) what
    c) who
    d) which

120 Before I accepted the new job offer, I talked it _____ with my wife.
a) in
b) over
c) about
d) out

121 I asked two people the way to the station but _____ of them knew.
a) no
b) either
c) both
d) neither

122 How long does it usually take to get _____ a cold?
a) better
b) recovered
c) over
d) out of

123 He's lazy. He never does _____ work.
a) any
b) some
c) no
d) the

124 I'm going to a wedding on Saturday. _____ is getting married.
a) A friend of me
b) A friend of mine
c) A friend of my
d) A friend of I

125 Housing costs in the southwest dropped slightly, _____, a survey showed that most people still consider a private home behind their means.
a) nevertheless
b) otherwise
c) therefore
d) so

126 My boss agreed _____ me have the day off.
a) letting
b) in let
c) to let
d) in letting

127 _____ regard to your transfer, I'm afraid it has been delayed.
a) Of
b) On
c) For
d) With

128   Billy and _____ will be working on Saturday morning.
 a) me
 b) I
 c) mine
 d) my

129   What time shall we _____ this evening?
 a) met
 b) meet
 c) meet us
 d) meet ourselves

130   They live on a busy road. _____ a lot of noise from the traffic.
 a) There must be
 b) It must be
 c) There must have
 d) It must have

131   Has Jeff stopped smoking for _____ or has he only quit for a month or so?
 a) now
 b) ever
 c) good
 d) long

132   The bus service is very good. There's a bus _____ ten minutes.
a) each
b) all
c) on each
d) every

133   Don't count _____ Jason to lend you any money because he has none.
a) in
b) with
c) on
d) over

134   With _____ did you have lunch?
a) whom
b) who
c) whose
d) which

135   I want to look _____ this exercises before I give them to the teacher.
a) after
b) over
c) up
d) back

136 How long did it take the firefighters to _____ out the fire?
a) take
b) put
c) run
d) make

137 I'm afraid the situation is getting _____.
a) worse
b) worst
c) worsen
d) worried

138 What time _____ on TV?
a) are news
b) is the news
c) are the news
d) is news

139 "The time is _____", the teacher said at the end of the test.
a) down
b) out
c) over
d) up

140 The teacher pointed _____ the mistakes in my composition.
   a) over
   b) in
   c) out
   d) down

141 Inflation last year was the _____ it has been since 2002.
   a) lowest
   b) lowed
   c) lower
   d) lowered

142 _____ my friend is 35 years old, he has never had a full-time job.
   a) Unless
   b) Because
   c) Although
   d) Since

143 He dug a deep _____ in the garden.
   a) hole
   b) haul
   c) whole
   d) hull

144   How long did it take you to figure_____ the cost of that new product?
   a) on
   b) down
   c) in
   d) out

145   Rough roads wear my tires _____.
   a) away
   b) out
   c) over
   d) off

146   Are you looking forward _____ Tom again?
   a) seeing
   b) seen
   c) to see
   d) to seeing

147   I'm tired. I'd rather _____ out this evening, if you don't mind.
   a) not go
   b) not going
   c) not to go
   d) don't go

148   John tried to be serious but he couldn't help _____.
   a) it laughing
   b) laughing
   c) to laugh
   d) that he laughed

149   Why does Grandma keep rocking back and _____
       in her chair?
   a) forward
   b) up
   c) forth
   d) front

150   I suddenly remember _____.
   a) who it was
   b) was it who
   c) who was it
   d) it who was

151   Who do you want to talk _____ ?
   a) with
   b) on
   c) to
   d) at

152   Which job has Tom applied _____?
    a) to
    b) for
    c) at
    d) with

153   Do you think is going to rain? _____.
    a) I'm hoping not
    b) I don't hope
    c) I don't hope so
    d) I hope not

154   The police officer stopped us and asked us where
    _____.
    a) we were going
    b) were we going
    c) are we going
    d) we are going

155   Do you know where _____ ? No, he didn't say.
    a) Mike is gone
    b) has Mike gone
    c) Mike has gone
    d) has gone Mike

156   How _____ ? Nobody knows.
   a)   does the accident happened
   b)   did the accident happen
   c)   happened the accident
   d)   did happen the accident

157   He's a reliable worker. He has never let me _____.
   a)   go down
   b)   yet
   c)   gone down
   d)   down yet

158   Look _____! A car is coming.
   a)   at
   b)   on
   c)   out
   d)   around

159   The check was made _____ to Brian Hoover.
   a)   out
   b)   over
   c)   on
   d)   in

160   That's not true. You're making it all _____.
        a) over
        b) up
        c) down
        d) in

161   Bob _____ and left.
        a) says goodbye
        b) said goodbye to me
        c) said me goodbye
        d) told me goodbye

162   I didn't expect to see you today. Dan said you
        _____ ill.
        a) were
        b) are
        c) should be
        d) where

163   I told him _____.
        a) not shouting
        b) don't shout
        c) shouldn't he shout
        d) not to shout

51

164   He asked me _____ anybody.
- a)   to don't tell
- b)   to not tell
- c)   not to tell
- d)   not tell to

165   What was the weather _____ yesterday?
- a)   on
- b)   there
- c)   here
- d)   like

166   Haven't we met _____ before?
- a)   sometimes
- b)   somewhere
- c)   somebody
- d)   someone

167   I don't know who _____ ?
- a)   that woman is
- b)   is that woman
- c)   woman is that
- d)   is that women

168   Do you know what time _____ ?
       a) is
       b) it is
       c) is it
       d) is now

169   I wish I _____ a car. It would make life so much
       easier.
       a) would have
       b) had
       c) have
       d) should have

170   If I were you, I _____ that coat. It's too expensive.
       a) won't buy
       b) don't buy
       c) am not going to buy
       d) wouldn't buy

171   I'm not tired enough to go to bed yet.
       I wouldn't sleep if I _____ to bed now.
       a) went
       b) go
       c) had gone
       d) would go

172   I decided to stay at home last night.
       I would have gone out if I _____ so tired.
       a) wouldn't have been
       b) wasn't
       c) hadn't been
       d) weren't

173   We don't have all day. Make _____ your mind, will
       you.
       a) on
       b) in
       c) over
       d) up

174   I'm going to sell my car to pay _____ my debts.
       a) off
       b) out
       c) away
       d) down

175   On Saturday you'll be the only one in the office.
       Don't forget to lock _____ before leaving.
       a) away
       b) over
       c) up
       d) out

176   Look _____ the children while we are out.
  a) on
  b) after
  c) at
  d) in

177   Don't worry _____ late tonight.
  a) when I'll be
  b) if I am
  c) when I am
  d) if I'll be

178   We're late. The movie _____ by the time we get to the cinema.
  a) will already have started
  b) will be ready to start
  c) will already start
  d) will be already started

179   The box looks heavy. _____ you with it.
  a) I'm helping
  b) I help
  c) I'll help
  d) I helped

180 _____ tomorrow, so we can go out somewhere.
   a) I can't work
   b) I don't work
   c) I won't work
   d) I'm not working

181 Stop harassing me! I don't have to put _____ with you.
   a) on
   b) over
   c) in
   d) up

182 Six dollars for a cup of coffee! This place is a rip _____.
   a) off
   b) on
   c) at
   d) over

183 We can't pay our bills. We're living _____ our means.
   a) around
   b) behind
   c) beyond
   d) under

184 He's late again. My patience is running _____.
   a) away
   b) out
   c) over
   d) down

185 It's two years _____ Mark.
   a) since I didn't see
   b) that I don't see
   c) since I saw
   d) that I haven't seen

186 She's my best friend. We _____ each other for a long time.
   a) have known
   b) know
   c) have been knowing
   d) knew

187 You're out of breath. _____ ?
   a) Are you running
   b) Have you been running
   c) Have you run
   d) Did you ran

188   Everything is going well. We _____ any problems
       so far.
       a) never had
       b) didn't have
       c) haven't had
       d) don't have

189   Can you tell me were _____ find John?
       a) I
       b) can I
       c) will I
       d) I can

190   Have you any idea how much _____ cost?
       a) it will
       b) it is
       c) will it
       d) it's

191   What time _____ the film begin?
       a) do
       b) had
       c) does
       d) has

192   Do you know if _____?
    a) anybody saw you
    b) anyone seen you
    c) anybody see you
    d) any saw you

193   I don't understand. What _____?
    a) does mean this word
    b) means this word
    c) does this word mean
    d) the word is meaning

194   She _____ her hand when she was cooking.
    a) got burning
    b) burnt
    c) was burning
    d) has burnt

195   Mark _____ tennis once a week.
    a) plays usually
    b) is playing usually
    c) is usually playing
    d) usually plays

196 It was a boring weekend. _____ anything.
   a) I don't do
   b) I didn't
   c) I didn't do
   d) I'm not doing

197 The neighborhood is dangerous. Watch _____ for thieves.
   a) in
   b) behind
   c) out
   d) around

198 It's a big problem but don't worry, we'll work it _____.
   a) on
   b) down
   c) over
   d) out

199 He's an incompetent salesman. He screwed _____ the hole deal.
   a) up
   b) around
   c) out
   d) away

200   Can you finish this _____ Friday?
   a) in
   b) by
   c) at
   d) over

201   Some of the people _____ to the party can't come.
   a) inviting
   b) invited
   c) who invited
   d) they were invited

202   Alex couldn't come to the party, _____ was a pity.
   a) that
   b) it
   c) what
   d) which

203   Peter told me about his new job, _____ very much.
   a) that he's enjoying
   b) which he's enjoying
   c) he's enjoying
   d) he's enjoying it

204   What's the name of the man _____ ?
   a) you borrowed his car
   b) which car you borrowed
   c) whose car you borrowed
   d) his car you borrowed

205   He asked me how old _____.
   a) I am
   b) was I
   c) am I
   d) I was

206   She wanted to know what _____ my spare time.
   a) I did in
   b) do I do
   c) I do on
   d) is done on

207   She asked me how long _____ been working in my present job.
   a) I have
   b) had I
   c) I had
   d) have I

208   He wanted to know whether _____ speak any
       foreign languages.
       a) I can
       b) I could
       c) can I
       d) could I

209   _____ she can't drive, she has bought a car.
       a) Even
       b) Even though
       c) Even if
       d) Even when

210   Tina _____. She left last month.
       a) doesn't work anymore here
       b) doesn't any more work here
       c) no more works here
       d) doesn't work here any more

211   _____ a long time for the bus.
       a) Always we have to wait
       b) We always have to wait
       c) We have always to wait
       d) We have to wait always

212 The movie was really boring. It was _____ I've ever
seen.
a) the most boring movie
b) the movie most boring
c) the more boring movie
d) most boring of movies

213 Charles admitted _____ the money.
a) having stolen
b) having stole
c) has stole
d) had steal

214 You can't stop me _____ I want.
a) to do what
b) on doing
c) doing what
d) in doing what

215 Sorry to _____ so long.
a) keep waiting you
b) keep you waiting
c) keep on waiting
d) keep waiting on

216   I now regret saying what _____.
    a) was saying
    b) I had say
    c) I said
    d) I say

217   They gave me a form and told me to _____.
    a) fill in
    b) fill it in
    c) fill in it
    d) fill it

218   I prefer coffee _____ tea.
    a) to
    b) than
    c) against
    d) over

219   What time will you arrive? I don't know. It depends _____ the traffic.
    a) of
    b) for
    c) from
    d) on

220   Who is John Adams? I've no idea. I've never heard
_____ him.
a) about
b) of
c) from
d) after

221   Alex has just found _____.
a) what does he think will be a very good job
b) what he thinks will be a very good job
c) a very good job he thinks will be
d) he thinks what will be a very good job

222   Please let me know _____.
a) when is it time to go
b) when time it is to go
c) when to go it is time
d) when it is time to go

223   The doctor has not yet determined _____.
a) what does Joe have
b) what Joe has
c) Joe has what
d) what has Joe

224 _____ incubating, a chicken's egg needs to be kept warm and dry.
   a) When it is
   b) Is it when
   c) It is when
   d) When is it

225 Not until several days after the accident _____ to remember what had happened.
   a) Peter began
   b) and Peter begun
   c) Peter beginning
   d) did Peter begin

226 Domestic cats enjoy playing and sitting in the sun, _____ _____ cats in the wild.
   a) and so do
   b) do so and
   c) so do and
   d) do and so

227 _____ that you borrowed his car, he would be very
angry.
a) Ever were Jack to find out
b) Were Jack ever to find out
c) Jack were ever to find out
d) Were ever to find out Jack

228 Through the woods _____ my uncle lives.
a) the house is where
b) where is the house
c) is the house where
d) where the house is

229 If you're worried about the problem, you should do something _____ it.
a) for
b) about
c) against
d) with

230 I'll be at home _____ Friday morning.
a) at
b) by
c) on
d) in

231   I'm not very good _____ repairing things.
       a) in
       b) about
       c) for
       d) at

232   Why are you so unfriendly _____ John?
       Have you had an argument with him?
       a) to
       b) of
       c) for
       d) with

233   Getting something is not always as easy as _____.
       a) wanting it
       b) when you want it
       c) to want it
       d) you want it

234   Frank spent the _____ day writing.
       a) hole
       b) haul
       c) whole
       d) hull

235   Car accidents are far more frequent than _____.
    a) having an accident in an airplane
    b) airplanes have accidents
    c) when there are plane accidents
    d) airplane accidents

236   Too much stress can cause sleeplessness, depression
    and _____.
    a) lack of appetite
    b) you don't want to eat
    c) lack of appetite is caused
    d) to lack appetite

237   He _____ my proposal.
    a) ejected
    b) rejected
    c) objected
    d) injected

238   You must _____ to vote 30 days before the elec-
    tion.
    a) sign
    b) submit
    c) register
    d) inquire

239   A huge project has been undertaken to _____ the
city's records.
a)   center
b)   centralize
c)   central
d)   centrally

240   She has a clear understanding of the various _____
of the case.
a)   facts
b)   information
c)   news
d)   knowledge

Section B

Section B

Circle the phrase that is closest in meaning (241-400)

241 Sarah got through that terrible performance somehow
   a) Sarah enjoyed it
   b) Sarah liked it
   c) Sarah endured it
   d) Sarah faked it

242 She always has been a go-getter
   a) She procrastinates
   b) She has few expectations
   c) She has a strong desire to succeed
   d) She always picks things up

243 Edward gave up when he didn't get the job
   a) Edward lost hope
   b) Edward was successful
   c) Edward got what he wanted
   d) Edward kept trying

244   Famous people are usually on their toes
   a) They are usually ill-prepared
   b) They are aware of the situation around them
   c) They lose hope easily
   d) They are in good shape

245   I have piles of work to do
   a) I have little work to do
   b) I have a lot of work to do
   c) I have to find something to do
   d) I have done a lot of work

246   Give me a dime
   a) Give me 25 cents
   b) Give me 5 cents
   c) Give me 10 cents
   d) Give me 50 cents

247   The water supply is safe
   a) The water provided is safe
   b) The water needed is safe
   c) The water requested is safe
   d) The water treated is safe

248   Your income decreased this year
    a) Your debts decreased this year
    b) The value of your property decreased this year
    c) Your payments decreased this year
    d) Your earnings decreased this year

249   They lost their belongings in the fire but they made the best of it
    a) They were depressed
    b) They benefited from the situation
    c) They were smart enough to recover
    d) They tried to be cheerful

250   Michael has set his sights on a new car
    a) Michael wants a new car
    b) Michael saw a new car
    c) Michael bought a new car
    d) Michael lost his new car

251   Neal couldn't keep up with them in the race
    a) Neal didn't stop
    b) Neal ran too fast
    c) Neal ran too slowly
    d) Neal didn't run

252 Why does she have it made?
   a) Why is she unsuccessful?
   b) Why is she done with it?
   c) Why is she successful?
   d) Why doesn't she get what she wants?

253 Roger died heavily in debt
   a) Roger died rich
   b) Roger died owning a lot of money
   c) Roger died leaving a lot of money
   d) Roger died owing a lot of money

254 I'm going to lease my place
   a) I'm going to sell my place
   b) I'm going to remodel my place
   c) I'm going to rent my place
   d) I'm going to lend my place

255 You should apply for a mortgage
   a) You should apply for a home loan
   b) You should apply for a car loan
   c) You should apply for a bank loan
   d) You should apply for a low interest loan

256   Tom lent me some money
    a) Tom gave me some money
    b) Tom borrowed some money from me
    c) I borrowed some money from Tom
    d) I gave Tom some money

257   Chris steered to the left
    a) Chris drove on the left
    b) Chris turned to the left
    c) Chris avoided the left
    d) Chris stayed away from the left

258   The plot was about love and marriage
    a) The course was about love and marriage
    b) The advice was about love and marriage
    c) The discussion was about love and marriage
    d) The story was about love and marriage

259   The product is at the design stage
    a) The product is being designed
    b) The product is in the design department
    c) The product is in a designed showroom
    d) A place was designed to show the product

260   We were given only two weeks to rehearse
   a)   We were given only two weeks to finish
   b)   We were given only two weeks to prepare
   c)   We were given only two weeks to rest
   d)   We were given only two weeks to recover

261   The police traced the call
   a)   The police made a call
   b)   The police answered the call
   c)   The police found the origin of the call
   d)   The police refused to answer the call

262   The ship vanished without a trace
   a)   The ship disappeared leaving no sign of its presence
   b)   The ship disappeared in the middle of nowhere
   c)   The ship disappeared quickly
   d)   The ship disappeared with no passengers on board

263   I'm looking for an ATM to make a withdrawal
   a)   I'm looking for an ATM to make a deposit
   b)   I'm looking for an ATM to get some cash
   c)   I'm looking for an ATM to make some cash
   d)   I'm looking for an ATM to cash a check

264   They have reached a settlement
    a) They have reached a climax
    b) They have reached a town
    c) They have reached the top of the mountain
    d) They have reached an agreement

265   Bruce signed up for the soccer team
    a) Bruce observed the team
    b) Bruce became a member of the team
    c) Bruce decided not to register for the team
    d) Bruce represented the team

266   Take your time when you eat
    a) Watch the clock when you eat
    b) Hurry when you eat
    c) Make sure you finish eating on time
    d) Don't hurry when you eat

267   They were uptight about the mortgage payments
    a) They were certain they got a good deal
    b) They had enough money for the payments
    c) They weren't certain they could afford the payments
    d) They knew they could afford the payments

268 They went through the inventory before purchasing the supplies
   a) They examined the inventory
   b) They forgot about the inventory
   c) They ignored the inventory
   d) They made an inventory

269 Jonathan is a close ally of the prime minister
   a) Jonathan is a rival of the prime minister
   b) Jonathan is a subordinate of the prime minister
   c) Jonathan is a relative of the prime minister
   d) Jonathan is a supporter of the prime minister

270 We must consider all the candidates without bias
   a) We must consider all the candidates impartially
   b) We must consider all the candidates with no defects
   c) We must consider all the candidates with no previous experience
   d) We must consider all the candidates with previous experience

271 She was able to hide in the wilderness
   a) She was able to hide in the hut
   b) She was able to hide in the forest
   c) She was able to hide in the barn
   d) She was able to hide under the sink

272   What's for dessert?
  a) What are we going to do with the arid areas?
  b) What sweet stuff are we eating after the meal?
  c) What can we do for the areas with no water?
  d) Are we going to snack before dinner?

273   He knows the poem by heart
  a) He memorized the poem
  b) He reads the poem from a book
  c) He forgot the poem
  d) He likes the poem

274   I'm off to the theater again
  a) I'm leaving the theater
  b) I'm still at the theater
  c) I'm going to the theater
  d) I'm out of the theater

275   Lisa knows her husband inside out
  a) Lisa understands him fairly well
  b) Lisa hardly understands him
  c) Lisa knows what he is doing outside
  d) Lisa understands him exceptionally well

276   The artist takes pains drawing pictures
    a) The artist is sloppy in his work
    b) The artist does meticulous work
    c) The artist draws until it hurts
    d) The artist draws carelessly

277   The drought is affecting the southwest
    a) Floods are affecting the southwest
    b) The lack of rain is affecting the southwest
    c) The rainy weather is affecting the southwest
    d) Heavy storms are affecting the southwest

278   Donna blushed when she saw him
    a) Donna frowned when she saw him
    b) Donna started crying when she saw him
    c) Donna showed her anger when she saw him
    d) Donna became red in the face when she saw him

279   I saw a child cringing in terror
    a) I saw a child shaking
    b) I saw a child screaming loudly
    c) I saw a scared child moving away
    d) I saw a worried child crying

280 It was a dim room
   a) It wasn't a well lighted room
   b) It was an insignificant room
   c) It was an uncomfortable room
   d) It wasn't a fancy room

281 It's filthy in here
   a) This place is very dangerous
   b) This place is very dirty
   c) This place is very expensive
   d) This place is frightening

282 The first half of the game was very dull
   a) The first half of the game was very exciting
   b) The first part of the game was disastrous
   c) The first part of the game was weird
   d) The first part of the game was boring

283 I screamed and everyone stared
   a) I screamed and everyone got upset
   b) I screamed and everyone ignored me
   c) I screamed and everyone told me to be quiet
   d) I screamed and everyone looked at me

284   There was a strange odor in the room
  a)   There was a strange old man in the room
  b)   There was a strange creature in the room
  c)   There was a strange smell in the room
  d)   There was a strange object in the room

285   He didn't move a muscle
  a)   He was lazy
  b)   He stood completely still
  c)   He didn't want to relax
  d)   He was weak

286   He's a very shrewd businessman
  a)   He's a very greedy businessman
  b)   He's a very nasty businessman
  c)   He's a very unreliable businessman
  d)   He's a very clever businessman

287   Where's the poultry section?
  a)   Where can I find the beef?
  b)   Where can I find the chicken?
  c)   Where can I find the fish?
  d)   Where can I find the jam?

288   The workmen were stripped to the waist
   a)   The workmen were wearing no shirts
   b)   The workmen were wearing no jackets
   c)   The workmen were wearing no underwear
   d)   The workmen were wearing no belts

289   They looked over their bills
   a)   They ignored them
   b)   They paid them
   c)   They examined them
   d)   They never received them

290   The nurse waited on the patient
   a)   The nurse helped the patient
   b)   The nurse was expecting the patient
   c)   The nurse left the patient
   d)   The nurse was looking for the patient

291   The boy got away with the stolen apples
   a)   He found the apples
   b)   He escaped with the apples
   c)   He was caught with the apples
   d)   He bought the apples

292   We settled on pizza for lunch
   a)   We prepared pizza for lunch
   b)   We served pizza for lunch
   c)   We rejected pizza for lunch
   d)   We decided to eat pizza for lunch

293   We're not hiring right now
   a)   We're not looking for suppliers
   b)   We're not employing people
   c)   We're not leasing
   d)   We're not looking for a job

294   These fish are often eaten raw
   a)   These fish are often eaten fresh
   b)   These fish are often eaten fried
   c)   These fish are often cooked with butter
   d)   These fish are often eaten uncooked

295   Robert devised a new system
   a)   Robert executed a new system
   b)   Robert located a new system
   c)   Robert thought up a new system
   d)   Robert fixed a new system

296   I was hired last year
    a)   I lost my position last year
    b)   I got the job last year
    c)   I got in trouble last year
    d)   I was sick last year

297   The refrigerator acts up during the hot summer months
    a)   It stops operating completely
    b)   It works just fine
    c)   It doesn't always work right
    d)   It operates better

298   She made up her mind to improve her education
    a)   She decided to improve her education
    b)   She wasn't sure about improving her education
    c)   She thought about improving her education
    d)   She knew it was possible to improve her education

299   Let's do without dessert
    a)   Let's eat dessert
    b)   Let's buy dessert
    c)   Let's consider eating dessert
    d)   Let's not eat dessert

300   He thought over repairing the car alone
    a)   He discussed repairing the car alone
    b)   He considered repairing the car alone
    c)   He wanted to repair the car alone
    d)   He talked about repairing the car alone

301   He scribbled on a scrap of paper
    a)   He scribbled on a document
    b)   He scribbled on a blank sheet of paper
    c)   He scribbled on a small piece of paper
    d)   He scribbled on a letter

302   It makes my heartache
    a)   It makes me sad
    b)   It makes my heat beat faster
    c)   It excites me
    d)   It makes me weak

303   Stephen fired me
    a)   Stephen lured me
    b)   Stephen sack me
    c)   Stephen burned me
    d)   Stephen liked me

304   Dick lacks confidence
        a) Dick doesn't have enough confidence
        b) Dick has too much confidence
        c) Dick has enough confidence
        d) Dick has a lot of confidence

305   Paul shoved her
        a) Paul picked her up
        b) Paul pushed her in a rough way
        c) Paul lifted her gently
        d) Paul squeezed her with his fingers

306   Don't be so nosy
        a) Don't be so inquisitive
        b) Don't be so aggressive
        c) Don't be so nasty
        d) Don't be so naïve

307   I like the façade of the building
        a) I like the interior of the building
        b) I like the front of the building
        c) I like the quality of the building
        d) I like the unique design of the building

308   This material is designed to absorb moisture
- a) It's designed to absorb dust
- b) It's designed to absorb poison
- c) It's designed to absorb humidity
- d) It's designed to absorb dirt

309   Jessica shouted at him
- a) Jessica angered him
- b) Jessica was trying to convince him
- c) Jessica spoke loudly to him
- d) Jessica rejected him

310   Nancy inhaled the warm moist air
- a) Nancy inhaled the warm dry air
- b) Nancy inhaled the warm slightly sour air
- c) Nancy inhaled the warm scented air
- d) Nancy inhaled the warm and slightly wet air

311   He's so naïve
- a) He's so innocent
- b) He's so unscrupulous
- c) He's so stubborn
- d) He's so nice

312 I coached her
   a) I practiced with her
   b) I learned from her
   c) I trained her
   d) I sat next to her

313 I achieved the goals
   a) I prepared the goals
   b) I set the goals
   c) I accomplished the goals
   d) I created the goals

314 The brown shoes go with the suit
   a) They contrast
   b) They match
   c) They are incompatible
   d) They are the same size

315 Jason backed me
   a) Jason hit me
   b) Jason ignored me
   c) Jason supported me
   d) Jason run away from me

316   The bakery was selling mouth-watering pies
    a)   The pies were stale
    b)   The pies were too sweet
    c)   The pies were tasteless
    d)   The pies were delicious

317   Those tomatoes are ripe
    a)   Those tomatoes are stale
    b)   Those tomatoes are too sour
    c)   Those tomatoes are ready to be eaten
    d)   Those tomatoes are spoiled

318   Donald enhanced his reputation
    a)   Donald smeared his reputation
    b)   Donald lost his reputation
    c)   Donald improved his reputation
    d)   Donald modified his reputation

319   Karen is outgoing
    a)   Karen is in a hurry
    b)   Karen is friendly
    c)   Karen is smart
    d)   Karen is very active

320   The cake has a thin coating of chocolate
    a) It has a thin layer of chocolate
    b) It has a thin wrap of chocolate
    c) It has a thin mix of chocolate
    d) It has a thin paste of chocolate

321   Because she was on the run, she forgot her keys
    a) Because she was running, she forgot her keys
    b) Because she was exercising, she forgot her keys
    c) Because she was speeding, she forgot her keys
    d) Because she was rushing, she forgot her keys

322   Preston loves to take it easy on the beach
    a) Preston loves to play with friends
    b) Preston loves to lie in the sun
    c) Preston loves to swim all day
    d) Preston loves to chase girls

323   Her relationship with her husband is on the mend
    a) It is at a standstill
    b) It is becoming worse
    c) It is improving
    d) It is not good

324   The movie will end before long
    a)   The movie will end shortly
    b)   The movie will end eventually
    c)   The movie will end later
    d)   The movie will end on time

325   These fish are found in shallow waters
    a)   These fish are found in clean waters
    b)   These fish are found in waters that aren't very deep
    c)   These fish are found in clear waters
    d)   These fish are found in very deep waters

326   Bulky items will be collected separately
    a)   Large items will be collected separately
    b)   Dangerous items will be collected separately
    c)   Small items will be collected separately
    d)   Thin items will be collected separately

327   This is going to be a huge problem for us
    a)   This is going to be a terrific problem for us
    b)   This is going to be a trivial problem for us
    c)   This is going to be a complicated problem for us
    d)   This is going to be a very big problem for us

328 That drink leaves a bitter taste in the mouth
   a) That drink leaves a slightly sweet taste in the mouth
   b) That drink leaves a pleasant taste in the mouth
   c) That drink leaves a strong unpleasant taste in the mouth
   d) That drink leaves a refreshingly cool taste in the mouth

329 I've had a rotten day
   a) I've had a terrific day
   b) I've had a busy day
   c) I've had a terrible day
   d) I've had a calm day

330 We need to add some spice to our lives
   a) We need to eat better food
   b) We need to add some excitement to our lives
   c) We need some peace and relaxation in our lives
   d) We need to stop worrying about everything

331 They have scrumptious desserts
   a) They have creamy desserts
   b) They have sweet desserts
   c) They have stale desserts
   d) They have delicious desserts

332   Susie is inquisitive
   a)   Susie is stubborn
   b)   Susie is intolerant
   c)   Susie is curious
   d)   Susie has good taste

333   Oliver is a suitable candidate
   a)   Oliver is an appropriate candidate
   b)   Oliver is an inadequate candidate
   c)   Oliver is a lousy candidate
   d)   Oliver is a lazy candidate

334   I'm reliable
   a)   I'm productive
   b)   I'm creative
   c)   I'm ingenious
   d)   I'm dependable

335   We arrived at dawn
   a)   We arrived at sunrise
   b)   We arrived at sunset
   c)   We arrived at noon
   d)   We arrived at midnight

336   We start work at daybreak
    a)   We start work at noon
    b)   We start work at sunset
    c)   We start work at dawn
    d)   We start work in the afternoon

337   They took care of the house while we were away
    a)   They stayed in the house
    b)   They left the doors and windows unlocked
    c)   They took things form the house
    d)   They made sure the house remained safe

338   They held the cooking class over for an hour
    a)   The class was in session for an extra hour
    b)   It was a one hour cooking class
    c)   The class started an hour late
    d)   They held the class in another place for an hour

339   Southern living is a change of pace from northern living
    a)   Southern living is similar to northern living
    b)   Southern living is better than northern living
    c)   Southern living is different from northern living
    d)   Southern living is the same as northern living

340   She's always on the go, and she loves it
   a)   She's always late
   b)   She's energetic
   c)   She's lazy
   d)   She's always on time

341   The pain was ebbing
   a)   The pain was decreasing
   b)   The pain was starting
   c)   The pain was increasing
   d)   The pain was excruciating

342   The pain in my back was excruciating
   a)   It was increasing
   b)   It was chronic
   c)   It was decreasing
   d)   It was unbearable

343   Fur seals were nearly wiped out a few years ago
   a)   They were nearly run over a few years ago
   b)   They were nearly taken away a few years ago
   c)   They were nearly exterminated a few years ago
   d)   They were nearly out of sight a few years ago

344   Stop whining
        a) Stop drinking wine
        b) Stop complaining
        c) Stop harassing people
        d) Stop interrupting

345   Steven is trustworthy
        a) Steven is reliable
        b) Steven is bright
        c) Steven is aggressive
        d) Steven is patient

346   Jack rose to his feet in a swift movement
        a) Jack rose to his feet in a slow movement
        b) Jack rose to his feet in a careful movement
        c) Jack rose to his feet in a precise movement
        d) Jack rose to his feet in a quick movement

347   The visitors got a chilly reception
        a) The visitors got a cordial reception
        b) The visitors got a proper reception
        c) The visitors got an unfriendly reception
        d) The visitors got a polite reception

348   Paul is very polite
   a)   Paul is very clever
   b)   Paul is very courteous
   c)   Paul is very temperamental
   d)   Paul is very nosy

349   It was a scary moment
   a)   It was an embarrassing moment
   b)   It was a frightening moment
   c)   It was a weird moment
   d)   It was an emotional moment

350   It was a creepy story
   a)   It was a boring story
   b)   It was a weird story
   c)   It was a very exciting story
   d)   It was a scary story

351   I didn't mean to frighten you
   a)   I didn't mean to scare you
   b)   I didn't mean to bore you
   c)   I didn't mean to make you cry
   d)   I didn't mean to let you down

352 Alice gave him a cuddle
- a) Alice kiss him gently
- b) Alice caressed him
- c) Alice hugged him
- d) Alice held his hand

353 His fingers caressed the back of her neck
- a) His fingers grabbed the back of her neck
- b) His fingers pushed the back of her neck
- c) His fingers pulled the back of her neck
- d) His fingers gently touched the back of her neck

354 Susan can be very prickly
- a) Susan can be very touchy
- b) Susan can be very sweet
- c) Susan can be very jealous
- d) Susan can be very shy

355 Scott is gregarious
- a) Scott is sociable
- b) Scott is shy
- c) Scott is quiet
- d) Scott is tenacious

356   The youth shook his shaggy head
    a)   The youth shook his lustrous head
    b)   The youth shook his shaven head
    c)   The youth shook his untidy head
    d)   The youth shook his round head

357   Gregory feels like leaving his job
    a)   Gregory feels good about his job
    b)   Gregory wants to keep his job
    c)   Gregory doesn't want to keep his job
    d)   Gregory doesn't want to be fired

358   He raved about her cooking
    a)   Her cooking was out of this world
    b)   Her cooking was terrible
    c)   Her cooking was mediocre
    d)   Her cooking wasn't terrific

359   At the age of thirty he was ready to settle down
    a)   He was ready to travel
    b)   He was ready to get married and stay in one place
    c)   He was ready to leave for an unknown destination
    d)   He was ready to open a new business

360   Darlene told the children to snap out of their foolishness
    a) Darlene told them to enjoy their foolishness
    b) Darlene told them to accept their foolishness
    c) Darlene told them to stop their foolishness
    d) Darlene told them not to end their foolishness

361   Howard spoke in a silky tone
    a) Howard spoke in a harsh tone
    b) Howard spoke in a loud and arrogant tone
    c) Howard spoke in a high pitch tone
    d) Howard spoke in a smooth and gentle tone

362   Derek annoys me
    a) Derek irritates me
    b) Derek helps me
    c) Derek makes me laugh
    d) Derek avoids me

363   It was a sly political move
    a) It was a clever political move
    b) It was a cunning political move
    c) It was a complicated political move
    d) It was a smart political move

364   Garry glanced at her slyly
- a) Garry glanced at her harshly
- b) Garry glanced at her playfully
- c) Garry glanced at her knowingly
- d) Garry glanced at her disdainfully

365   Dennis was a small-time crook
- a) Dennis was a petty crook
- b) Dennis was a dangerous crook
- c) Dennis was a clever crook
- d) Dennis was a young crook

366   They had small-town views
- a) They had strong views
- b) They had solid views
- c) They had interesting views
- d) They had narrow-minded views

367   The last few words of the letter were smeared
- a) The last few words of the letter were sharp
- b) The last few words of the letter were smudged
- c) The last few words of the letter were erased
- d) The last few words of the letter were highlighted

368   Ted tried to smother a yawn
    a) Ted tried to avoid a yawn
    b) Ted tried to stifle a yawn
    c) Ted tried to cover a yawn
    d) Ted tried to simulate a yawn

369   It was a blurred image
    a) It was a sharp image
    b) It was a complex image
    c) It was a colorful image
    d) It was a smudgy image

370   It was a snug little house
    a) It was a cozy little house
    b) It was a dirty little house
    c) It was a strange little house
    d) It was a scary little house

371   Betty is eager for her parents' approval
    a) Betty is not worried about her parents' approval
    b) Betty is keen for her parents' approval
    c) Betty is expecting her parents' approval
    d) Betty is not used to her parents' approval

372   Sylvia spoke words full of venom and gall
   a) Sylvia spoke words full of venom and mystery
   b) Sylvia spoke words full of venom and sadness
   c) Sylvia spoke words full of venom and resentment
   d) Sylvia spoke words full of venom and grace

373   Allen is weighed down with guilt
   a) Allen is burden with guilt
   b) Allen is conscious with guilt
   c) Allen is covered with guilt
   d) Allen is able to deal with guilt

374   The injured man was lying on the ground, moaning
   a) The injured man was lying on the ground, bluffing
   b) The injured man was lying on the ground, crying
   c) The injured man was lying on the ground, shaking
   d) The injured man was lying on the ground, groaning

375   Wade pleases me
   a) Wade asks for favors
   b) Wade satisfies me
   c) Wade bothers me
   d) Wade worries me

376   Richard is going to prune a rose bush
    a)   Richard is going to turn down a rose bush
    b)   Richard is going to plant a rose bush
    c)   Richard is going to water a rose bush
    d)   Richard is going to cut back a rose bush

377   Juliet was offered the leading role in the new TV series
    a)   Juliet was offered the latest role
    b)   Juliet was offered the most demanding role
    c)   Juliet was offered the best role
    d)   Juliet was offered the main role

378   Henry is a person with socialist leanings
    a)   Henry is a person with socialist relatives
    b)   Henry is a person with socialist inclinations
    c)   Henry is a person with socialist studies
    d)   Henry is a person with socialist connections

379   They are talking about his lewd behavior
    a)   They are talking about his obscene behavior
    b)   They are talking about his weird behavior
    c)   They are talking about his aggressive behavior
    d)   They are talking about his strange behavior

380   Summon a conference
    a)   Cancel a conference
    b)   Give a conference
    c)   Convene a conference
    d)   Review a conference

381   Dad will be livid when he finds out
    a)   Dad will be surprised when he finds out
    b)   Dad will be very proud when he finds out
    c)   Dad will be furious when he finds out
    d)   Dad will be embarrassed when he finds out

382   Teenagers were loitering
    a)   Teenagers were driving to fast
    b)   Teenagers were stealing
    c)   Teenagers were fighting
    d)   Teenagers were hanging around

383   The food was only lukewarm
    a)   The food was just fine
    b)   The food was enough to keep you alive
    c)   The food was only tepid
    d)   The food was succulent

384   I've had a lousy day
   a) I've had a boring day
   b) I've had an awful day
   c) I've had a fascinating day
   d) I've had an exciting day

385   Neil made out that he had been robbed
   a) Neil knew that he had been robbed
   b) Neil thought that he had been robbed
   c) Neil acknowledged that he had been robbed
   d) Neil claimed that he had been robbed

386   It's a private matter
   a) It's a private property
   b) It's a private situation
   c) It's a private affair
   d) It's a private place

387   I managed to do it
   a) I was in charge of it
   b) I was able to do it
   c) I was in control of it
   d) I used my skills to do it

388   She's always been mean with money
   a)   She's always been stingy
   b)   She's always been nasty
   c)   She's always been rude
   d)   She's always been bad with numbers

389   Bryan has a menacing face
   a)   Bryan has a handsome face
   b)   Bryan has a cute face
   c)   Bryan has a threatening face
   d)   Bryan has a ugly face

390   It's a nuisance having to go back tomorrow
   a)   It's exciting having to go back tomorrow
   b)   It's a waste of time having to go back tomorrow
   c)   It's terrific having to go back tomorrow
   d)   It's annoying having to go back tomorrow

391   Andy is shrewd
   a)   Andy is clever
   b)   Andy is creative
   c)   Andy is businesslike
   d)   Andy is loyal

392 Mary has inherited her mother's stubborn streak
   a) Mary has inherited her mother's beauty
   b) Mary has inherited her mother's obstinate streak
   c) Mary has inherited her mother's shyness
   d) Mary has inherited her mother's clever streak

393 I managed to stutter a reply
   a) I managed to find a reply
   b) I managed to avoid a reply
   c) I managed to whisper a reply
   d) I managed to stammer a reply

394 Protective clothing is compulsory
   a) Protective clothing is necessary
   b) Protective clothing is recommendable
   c) Protective clothing is obligatory
   d) Protective clothing is useful

395 The pain was almost more than he could bear
   a) The pain was almost more than he could expect
   b) The pain was almost more than he could stand
   c) The pain was almost more than he could think
   d) The pain was almost more than he could fear

396   This is a problem that beats even the experts
    a)   This is a problem that defeats even the experts
    b)   This is a problem that puzzles even the experts
    c)   This is a problem that challenges even the experts
    d)   This is a problem that intrigues even the experts

397   It was not a very becoming behavior for a teacher
    a)   It was not a very unusual behavior for a teacher
    b)   It was not a very eccentric behavior for a teacher
    c)   It was not a very peculiar behavior for a teacher
    d)   It was not a very fitting behavior for a teacher

398   Beverly has a flawless complexion
    a)   Beverly has a perfect complexion
    b)   Beverly has a nice complexion
    c)   Beverly has a untidy complexion
    d)   Beverly has a dry complexion

399   These plants thrive in a dump climate
    a)   These plants are difficult to find in a dump climate
    b)   These plants can't grow in a dump climate
    c)   These plants flourish in a dump climate
    d)   These plants die in a dump climate

400   The President was compelled to resign
    a) The President was trying to resign
    b) The President was forced to resign
    c) The President was unable to resign
    d) The President was happy to resign

Answer key

Answer key

001 a	018 c	035 d
002 b	019 a	036 c
003 c	020 c	037 c
004 d	021 c	038 d
005 a	022 c	039 a
006 b	023 a	040 b
007 d	024 d	041 b
008 c	025 c	042 a
009 b	026 a	043 c
010 b	027 d	044 d
011 d	028 c	045 c
012 d	029 c	046 b
013 b	030 d	047 a
014 a	031 b	048 d
015 d	032 a	049 c
016 c	033 c	050 b
017 d	034 b	051 b

052 a	073 d	094 a
053 c	074 c	095 c
054 a	075 b	096 b
055 d	076 d	097 d
056 c	077 b	098 d
057 c	078 c	099 b
058 d	079 a	100 c
059 b	080 d	101 a
060 a	081 b	102 d
061 b	082 c	103 d
062 b	083 a	104 c
063 d	084 d	105 b
064 a	085 a	106 d
065 d	086 d	107 d
066 a	087 b	108 a
067 b	088 c	109 b
068 c	089 d	110 c
069 d	090 b	111 d
070 a	091 a	112 b
071 b	092 c	113 d
072 b	093 a	114 c

115 b	136 b	157 d
116 c	137 a	158 c
117 a	138 b	159 a
118 c	139 d	160 b
119 d	140 c	161 b
120 b	141 a	162 a
121 d	142 c	163 d
122 c	143 a	164 c
123 a	144 d	165 d
124 b	145 b	166 b
125 a	146 d	167 a
126 c	147 a	168 b
127 d	148 b	169 b
128 b	149 c	170 d
129 b	150 a	171 a
130 a	151 c	172 c
131 c	152 b	173 d
132 d	153 d	174 a
133 c	154 a	175 c
134 a	155 c	176 b
135 b	156 b	177 b

178 a	199 a	220 b
179 c	200 b	221 b
180 d	201 b	222 d
181 d	202 d	223 b
182 a	203 b	224 a
183 c	204 c	225 d
184 b	205 d	226 a
185 c	206 a	227 b
186 a	207 c	228 c
187 b	208 b	229 b
188 c	209 b	230 c
189 d	210 d	231 d
190 a	211 b	232 a
191 c	212 a	233 a
192 a	213 a	234 c
193 c	214 c	235 d
194 b	215 b	236 a
195 d	216 c	237 b
196 c	217 b	238 c
197 c	218 a	239 b
198 d	219 d	240 a

241 c	262 a	283 d
242 c	263 b	284 c
243 a	264 d	285 b
244 b	265 b	286 d
245 b	266 d	287 b
246 c	267 c	288 a
247 a	268 a	289 c
248 d	269 d	290 a
249 d	270 a	291 b
250 a	271 b	292 d
251 c	272 b	293 b
252 c	273 a	294 d
253 d	274 c	295 c
254 c	275 d	296 b
255 a	276 b	297 c
256 c	277 b	298 a
257 b	278 d	299 d
258 d	279 c	300 b
259 a	280 a	301 c
260 b	281 b	302 a
261 c	282 d	303 b

304 a	325 b	346 d
305 b	326 a	347 c
306 a	327 d	348 b
307 b	328 c	349 b
308 c	329 c	350 d
309 c	330 b	351 a
310 d	331 d	352 c
311 a	332 c	353 d
312 c	333 a	354 a
313 c	334 d	355 a
314 b	335 a	356 c
315 c	336 c	357 c
316 d	337 d	358 a
317 c	338 a	359 b
318 c	339 c	360 c
319 b	340 b	361 d
320 a	341 a	362 a
321 d	342 d	363 b
322 b	343 c	364 c
323 c	344 b	365 a
324 a	345 a	366 d

367 b	379 a	391 a
368 b	380 c	392 b
369 d	381 c	393 d
370 a	382 d	394 c
371 b	383 c	395 b
372 c	384 b	396 a
373 a	385 d	397 d
374 d	386 c	398 a
375 b	387 b	399 c
376 d	388 a	400 b
377 d	389 c	
378 b	390 d	

COLECCIÓN DIDÁCTICA

Antropología simplificada
Curso elemental de psicología
Conoce a los dinosaurios
Elementos de sociología
Estudiantes de éxito
Inglés avanzado superfácil
Inglés en XX lecciones
Inglés en modismos
Inglés para niños
Inglés sin maestro para ejecutivos
Inglés sin maestro para estudiantes
Inglés super fácil
Juega en inglés
Pronunciación del inglés super fácil
Lectura super rápida
Lógica ilógica
Los niños salvaremos la tierra
La magia como herramienta de enseñanza
Nomenclatura química inorgánica
Super lectura para estudiantes
Tae kwon do para niños
Tae kwon do para principiantes
Toefl -Ejercicios prácticos para el examen-

COLECCIONES

Aguaviva
Belleza
Negocios
Superación personal
Salud
Familia
Literatura infantil
Literatura juvenil
Ciencia para niños
Con los pelos de punta
Pequeños valientes
¡Que la fuerza te acompañe!
Juegos y acertijos
Manualidades
Cultural
Clásicos para niños
Didáctica
Esoterismo
Historia para niños
Historias de la Biblia
Humorismo
Interés general
Cocina
Inspiracional
Ajedrez
B. Traven
Biografías para niños
Clásicos juveniles
Sueños
México Mágico
Chequeras
Novela
Mis valores

Esta edición se imprimió en Abril 2011 en Ares Impresiones
Sabino No. 12 Col. El Manto. Iztapalapa